A Puppy Love Guide

*About the German Shepherd,
Tips for Bringing your GSD Pup Home,
and Doggone Delicious Recipes*

Virginia Clark

eBook

Copyright 2016

All Rights Reserved

ASIN: B01CKHIMPA

Requests for information should be addressed to:

A Vegas Publisher, LLC.

www.avegaspublisher.com

avegaspublisher@gmail.com

                First edition: 2016

Cover Design: Virginia Clark

Interior Design: Virginia Clark

Photography furnished by: Virginia Clark

Images provided by: Virginia Clark

Part I

About The German Shepherd

The German shepherd, commonly abbreviated GSD for German shepherd dog, is the second most popular breed, according to the American Kennel Club, behind the Labrador retriever. Their courage, lifelong devotion, loyalty, confidence, ability to learn, and willingness to protect their owners far excels any other breed. They are eager to have a purpose, are quick to learn, and interpret tasks and instructions with ease.

Their many endearing traits also include, but not limited to, their steady demeanor, versatility, adeptness, obedience, and companionship. They are athletic, protective, courageous, highly trainable, sociable, alert, and watchful. Their most endearing trait, because of their versatility, is they make for the ideal choice as a family pet.

The origin of the breed dates back to 1899 and is credited to Max von Stephanitz, known as the Father of the Modern German shepherd. A career cavalry officer, Stephanitz served at the Berlin Veterinary College where he gained extensive knowledge in anatomy and biology which he then began to apply to the breeding of dogs. His primary interest was improving the local German shepherd dog because he believed he could create a better working dog and in the process, attempt to create a standardization of the breed.

In 1899, joined with several co-founders, Stephanitz founded the Verein für Deutsche Schäferhunde (S.V.), a society for the German shepherd dog. They developed a breed evaluation test developed specifically for the German shepherd dog called the Schutzhund Test (Schutzhund is the German word meaning "protection dog"). The purpose of this test is to measure the dog's mental stability, endurance, structural efficiencies, ability to scent, willingness to work, courage, and trainability. The conclusion of the test is to identify whether or not the dog has desirable traits in tracking, obedience, and protection to perform well as a military or police dog when making its debut during the First World War. Still in existence today, there are hundreds of Schutzhund Clubs worldwide.

    The German shepherd is working dog and they were originally bred to herd and guard sheep, and to protect flocks from predators, henceforth "shepherd" in its name. Von Stephanitz originally named the breed "Deutscher Schaferhund", which translates as "German shepherd dog". Due to anti- German sentiment at the conclusion of World War I, the name "German" was considered harmful to the popularity of the breed and was re named "Alsatian Wolf Dog". In 1977, pressured by dog enthusiasts, the breed became known as the German shepherd worldwide.

    Being a very popular choice as a working dog, the German shepherd plays an active role in many situations because of their keen sense of smell and astute focus. They are used as police, military, and guard dogs. They are trained as guide dogs, search and rescue, narcotics detection, cadaver searching, explosive and accelerant detection. They are used for security in airports, in places of large assembly for crowd control, detection and apprehension. They serve well as therapy, and service dogs. There are many applications of use for this breed.

The average height and weight of a German shepherd male is 24" to 26" tall and ranging from 66 to 88 pounds; the average height and weight for a female is 22" to 24" tall and ranging from 49 to 71 pounds. This is the average height and weight and it is possible for them to be larger in size, but unlikely to be smaller than the average measurements. The average life span is 9 to 13 years and some have been known to live even longer depending on the quality of health.

German shepherds come in a variety of colors. The most common colors are black and tan, and black and red. Rare color variations include all black, and sable. There are also liver, blue, and all white colors which are not acceptable according to the standards; they are considered serious faults which can be contest disqualified although these colors do not indicate the dog is substandard by any means.

German shepherds are known for being television stars because of their acute trainability. The most famous dog was Rin TinTin and he even has a star on the Hollywood Walk of Fame. At the peak of his career, he received 10,000 pieces of fan mail per week! Other famous shepherds include London who appeared in The Littlest Hobo; Ace the Wonder Dog appeared in numerous shows in the 1930's through the 1940's; Bullet appeared in the Roy Rogers Show in the 1950's; Jerry Lee appeared with James Belushi in the movie K-9; and Rusty appeared in The Rusty series during the 1950's.

Caring for him needs to include daily activity to achieve maximum physical and mental stimulation. This breed needs to run, play, burn off energy, and learn.

Their minds are like a sponge and absorb knowledge rapidly. These dogs want to please their owners and need a steady activity routine to reach their full potential. A bored dog is apt to dig, chew, and become destructive.

Known to be workaholics, they will exhaust themselves playing and will not stop until you end the playing and learning sessions. Do not be fooled into thinking that because you have a dog you do not need to provide training. German shepherds enjoy training and quite often excel in the training classes. Just remember to play with your puppy for the first two years on soft surfaces, such as grass or rubber mats, and keep jumps low until it is fully grown and its joints are fully formed. A German shepherd is fully grown by three years of age.

Be sure to have plenty of sturdy toys on hand for your dog to play with because they love their toys, especially balls! Just be sure to use sturdy balls, not tennis balls. A German shepherd can easily skin a tennis ball and break the ball in half. Once broken in half, the tennis ball becomes a choking hazard.

They love food and love to eat. It is easy for your adult dog to become overweight if you do not monitor their diet. Depending on its size, metabolism, and activity level, you should feed the recommended daily amount of 1 1/2 cups of high quality dry food twice a day. If you have a very active dog, then raise the amount to 2 cups of food twice a day. Limit treats as rewards when training and playing. To be sure your dog is not overweight; place your hands on its back with your thumbs along the spine with fingers spread downwards. You should be able to feel the ribs without pressing too hard. You should also be able to see the slight hourglass waist.

If you cannot feel the ribs nor see the waist, then you need to reduce the amount of food to 1 cup fed twice a day and increase your exercise regime. When he is still a puppy, be certain to feed a high quality dry food diet to promote proper growth and development and continue this program for a full year.

Grooming your GSD is easy and you'll find they enjoy being groomed. They are double-coated, that means the weather resistant undercoat is soft and downy while the outer coat is a coarser, weather-repellant guard coat. The outer coat sheds year round and the thick, protective undercoat sheds minimally. Because they do shed moderately, The German shepherd is jokingly referred to as a "German shredder". It is not recommended to shave the coat.

The breed is not considered to be a water dog, however many love water and their webbed feet make swimming easy. Washing your dog will be pleasurable because they will enjoy playing in the water at bath time. During bath time, be sure to wash the outer ears to avoid getting ear infections. You should check its ears weekly for any indications of infections such as redness or foul odor.

Often overlooked is brushing a dog's teeth and you need to remember to brush the teeth at least three times a week or more.

Trimming nails is another overlooked grooming necessity. If you can hear the nails clicking on the floor, then they need to be trimmed. Active dogs naturally wear their nails down, but older, less active dogs do not.

If you have purchased your puppy from a reliable, experienced breeder, then you should have a healthy puppy, but there are no guarantees as your puppy grows into an adult dog. Cancer rates are one of the highest health risks to the German shepherd. In a study by The Orthopedic Foundation for Animals (OFA) 41% of dogs reported as deceased died of cancer.

Other health risks associated with this breed include, but not limited to:

- Osteochondrosis of the Elbow/Ankle/Knee/Spine: Small cracks in the cartilage lead to a lifting or separation of the cartilage into the joint, thereby compromising the smooth movements we expect from the dogs' joints. Pain from the rubbing caused by the presence of this abnormal cartilage is the inevitable result. The joints of the elbow, knee and ankle are most commonly affected, though lesions like this have been seen in the spine. Limping in one or both hind limbs is the most common sign. Affected dogs may not experience pain, while others will. They may only have trouble upon rising or appear stiff when they walk and run. X-Rays and CT scans can accurately diagnose this condition.

- Hip and Elbow Dysplasia:
Hip and elbow dysplasia is a genetic disease that causes mild to severe changes to the inner workings of the hip and elbow. It is considered the most common of all orthopedic diseases in large dogs. To be more specific about hip and elbow

dysplasia, the ball portion of the hip or elbow does not align in the socket properly causing the joint to erode. Both hip and elbow dysplasia is painful and expensive to treat. It is not always obvious that your dog has it and some signs indicate the condition as early as four months of age while others may not see signs until their dog reaches middle age or older. As your dog ages, the end result becomes crippling arthritis, also referred to as osteoarthritis. Some indications that your dog may have hip or elbow dysplasia is limping, loss of muscle mass, walking differently, reluctance to jumping, and slowness when rising. Your veterinarian can perform X-rays to identify the problem and access the quality of your dog's hip or elbow. The best way to minimize the possibility of your dog getting hip and elbow dysplasia is to ask your breeder to show you the results of the X-rays of the pup's parents and to ask about the presence of hip or elbow dysplasia in the litter's lineage.

- Cardiomyopathy:
Genetics is presumed to cause the inability of the cardiac muscles to contract properly, known as Cardiomyopathy. This means that the amount of blood pumped by the heart is decreased, leading to poor circulation and secondary effects on the unaffected heart muscles. Canines who acquire this condition are usually large breed dogs and they generally do so during or after middle age and the condition does vary by breed. Due to electrical conduction, the disease is characterized by collapse and weakness of cardiac muscles and sudden death can result from the stretching or compensation of the heart muscle. The most typical indications of Cardiomyopathy include coughing and

difficulty breathing, but the most common indication is a heart murmur. X-Rays and EKG's can provide a diagnosis of this disease.

- Bloat:

The proper medical term is Gastric Dilatation Volvulus and means a sudden accumulation of stomach gas and the twisting of the stomach. This is a very serious condition and required immediate medical attention. As the blood vessels become twisted in the stomach, the end result is irreversible stomach death, shock, and the release of deadly toxins in the blood stream. Symptoms should not be ignored if you witness dry-retching, nausea, abdominal distension, and restlessness. The vet will take x-rays and bloodwork to diagnose the condition and emergency surgery will be ordered. The survival rate is low if deadly toxins have been released into the system and damaged other organs. Some preventative measures are possible to eliminate Bloat, but this does not necessarily that your dog will not suffer from this condition: avoid grain based pet food, feed your dog small to medium size raw bones regularly, do not exercise your dog for three hours after eating, be sure the diet consists of essential nutrients, use feeding stations leveled at chest height so your dog is not leaning down into the bowl to eat or drink, and always be sure you have plenty of fresh water available.

- Degenerative Myelopaty
Commonly referred to as DM, this appears frequently in the German shepherd. This auto-immune disorder is the destruction of the central nervous system. An indication your dog may have this disorder is recognized by abnormally worn nails of the hind paw, dragging of the hind paw, no control of the rear limb

direction and posterior weakness. Consult your veterinarian for a diagnosis; there is no cure for this disease but supplements can be administered to ease the condition.

- Canine Epilepsy

Possibly transmitted genetically, Canine Epilepsy begins to express itself between three and four years of age. The recurrent seizures refer to the involuntary contractions of muscles caused by an electrical storm within the brain. It is considered a broad and diverse disorder due to a variety of causes. Some causes can be the result of brain tumors, head trauma, low or high blood sugar, electrolyte imbalance, hypothyroidism, infection, liver disease, kidney failure, severe worm infestation, cancer, poisoning, vitamin deficiencies, and ingestion of lead. There is no way to diagnose the condition until your dog has a seizure. A seizure can last from one minute to more than five minutes and can leave your dog confused, disoriented, and exhausted. Your dog may experience sudden violent shaking, stiffness, urinating, salivating, and could lose consciousness. To help your vet correctly diagnose Canine Epilepsy, you need to thoroughly document all you have witnessed when a seizure occurs. During a seizure you need to remain calm and avoid the mouth and head area so you do not get inadvertently bitten. Dogs cannot swallow their tongues, so do not put anything in its mouth. If possible, time the length of the seizure for reporting to your vet. A seizure can cause your dog to overheat quickly; once the seizure has ended you need to cool your pet by placing the paws in cool water and placing a fan on your dog. Once the seizure has ended, call your vet. A thorough examination and lab work will be preformed to diagnose the condition with accuracy. Prescriptions such as Phenobarbital or potassium bromide can help control the condition and you need to be mindful to not miss a dose.

Part II

Transition from Kennel to Home

As a pre-eminent breeder of German shepherds, I am often asked questions and opinions on caring for a puppy once it goes home. Many first time dog owners have so many questions on proper care and what to do in certain situations. I have learned so much over the years and feel highly qualified to properly address many questions and concerns about many breeds, not just German shepherds. As fun as it is getting a new puppy, it can be overwhelming at the same time. The transition from the kennel to the home can be tricky.

    I have compiled the most commonly asked questions to help ease your concerns on being a new puppy owner. Once you master the basics of proper care, you will find yourself completely at ease with your new puppy. You will fall in love with your new puppy, and you'll proudly embrace all the milestones your puppy has achieved.

The most important thing to remember is to remain in control of your dog, not to have your dog control you. You'll learn the benefits of praise and reward, and work hand-in-hand with your new pup while being consistent with positive reinforcement. Bringing your new puppy home is so exciting! I hope you thoroughly enjoy your puppy love!

Bringing your puppy home

For the purposes of not repeating "your puppy" throughout the book, we're using a generic "he" or "him" (with no intended slight for the ladies out there) for some of the repetitive phrases. Going home with your new pup is an exciting time for you and your family, but it can be a bit overwhelming for him. Starting with the car ride from the kennel to your home, your eight-week-old puppy will be nervous. You have to look at this from the pups' perspective to understand the anxiety he feels. Complete strangers just came and took him away from the comfort and familiarity of the only home they know.

Missing their mother, fellow litter mates and breeder, combined with the motion of the car could make your puppy sick. Two people should pick up the pup from the kennel: one as a driver and the other to hold and comfort him. Plan to have towels on hand just in case your pup does vomit or void on your lap.

This is a natural reaction to this situation, and you should not scold him for this. When we picked up Shelby from the kennel and brought her home, I was not properly prepared. I was so excited to pick her up, I forgot my supplies. She did vomit all over me, all over the car, and all over the dashboard. It was most unpleasant and all of this could have been avoided if I had planned ahead. It took weeks to get the smell out of the car as an added bonus to my forgetfulness.

What to expect once you are home with your new puppy

Arriving home will continue to be stressful for him, and your calmness and patience will ease the transition for him from the kennel to your home. Coming home with your new animal is exciting! You have waited for this day to arrive, you have all your supplies ready, and your friends and family all share in your excitement and cannot wait to meet him or her. This is not the time to invite people over, no matter how excited you are to show everyone the newest member of the family. This should not be about your excitement at this particular place in time; it should be all about your puppy and the ease of transition into the new environment. Ask visitors to come a week or two after your pup has had time to adjust to the new home and family. Once you allow people to visit, please ask everyone to remove their shoes and wash their hands prior to being introduced. The puppy will be quite young still and not have all the required vaccinations. It takes nearly seven months to get all their shots. This means your puppy is vulnerable to becoming sick by coming in contact with germs, possible parasites, and other contaminants. For this same reason, you should not introduce the new puppy to other animals other than the pets that are already established in your home until he is fully inoculated.

Removal of the shoes is most important because this is how Giardia, worms, and Parvo can be transferred into your home. Parvo is lethal, and you do not want to risk the life of your pup by not taking the proper steps to ensure his health and safety. Parvo is transferred from one animal to another through feces. If a person stepped on contaminated feces, the microorganism will be transferred to your home from the shoes. Parvo can kill the new pup in less than five days. It is treatable, but the success rate is very low for newbie's and elderly dogs alike. Parvo is a hearty, highly contagious virus and can thrive in any environment for years, undetected, while waiting for a new host.

Case in point: We had a healthy, beautiful female puppy leave the kennel at eight weeks of age. During her stay with us, the adoptive family moved into their home and prepared for the arrival of their new puppy. Little did they know the previous homeowners had a dog that was sick with the Parvo virus. Even though the yard was feces-free, the virus continued to thrive in the ground. Once the new puppy was introduced to the yard, she picked up the virus. Two days after sweet baby Abita left our kennel, she was vomiting and had severe diarrhea. They took her to the vet and found out she was infected. Abita never had a chance to live and she, not-so-quietly, passed away. It was rough; gut wrenching, and terribly sad for all of us and especially sad for the three-year-old toddler that did not understand what happened to her new puppy that she loved so much.

Now that you have your new puppy at home, you should allow 24 hours of transition time. I tell everyone to let their puppy roam around, sniff, explore and do whatever it wants in order to adjust to the new environment on its own terms. I, too, follow this rule of logic. As an example, we recently acquired another female to breed when she becomes of age. She was so frightened when she came into the house that she ran under a table to hide.

I let her stay there and went about my business. I knew eventually she would creep out from under the table to explore. It took several hours, but once she did emerge on her own terms she was no longer frightened, and she began to warm up to the house, her fellow mates, and us.

After the first 24 hours have passed, begin to get your new puppy into a routine. This routine should be exactly what the definition of routine is: a sequence of actions regularly followed: a fixed program. Your routine should include feeding times, potty times, playtimes, bedtime, and any other actions or activities you would like to introduce to your puppy. A dog with a routine tends to be more obedient.

It is not uncommon for your puppy to cry at night for the first few days. This is a time when he will feel the loneliness and the separation anxiety that comes with leaving the kennel. You may not get much rest, you may feel frustrated, and you may want to yell at your puppy to "Go to sleep." Do not, under any circumstance, yell at him during this time. It does not speak your language yet and does not understand what you're saying. The puppy will associate your negative attention as positive attention. The crying will be prolonged if you pay any attention. Do not rock your puppy to sleep. Do not bring the puppy to bed with you. Do not do anything! I know this appears cruel and perhaps wrong, but trust this advice because it works. If you have a puppy with a dominant personality, he will vie for attention and cry to get its own way.

My personal experience occurred when we got Duke at 8 weeks of age. Duke was exhibiting alpha male tendencies at this very early age. He was determined to emerge as the leader of the pack, ahead of me. He wanted to express his dominance. Every night he would cry, cry, cry, and then cry some more. I was frustrated and exhausted. I just wanted to sleep! I called the vet to ask if something was wrong with him, and she told me that I should ignore him, the same advice just discussed. So I ignored him night after night. This went on for several weeks, and by that time I was at wits end. Then suddenly I woke one morning and realized he had been quiet all night! We all got sleep! It was wonderful! From that time forward, I realized I won the battle of the night-time crying, and I became the dominant force, not Duke. Duke has been a charm ever since and sleeps beside me on the floor, ever vigilant and silently protecting me.

A family that bought one of our pups called me because her puppy was doing the same crying all night. The woman was upset that this was happening and thought something was wrong with her puppy. I gave her the same advice on what to do, and although she thought the idea sounded a bit preposterous, she did agree to give this a try. She followed my advice and called me back a week later and told me all was well with the night-time crying, and Obi was finally sleeping soundly.

Keep in mind this does not happen with all pups. Some do not cry at all; some cry for just a day or two. If you should be the person that has one that cries, you now know how to effectively handle the situation.

Introducing a baby

Properly introducing your new puppy to an infant is an important part of knowing how the puppy will react currently and in the future, and it must be done slowly. If you are not sure how the new puppy will react, you should introduce them while another adult is present and one of you is holding the leash. Begin by holding clothing your infant has worn, and let the puppy sniff the garment to get familiar with the scent. You want him to feel positive about the baby, allow him to become familiar with the scent prior to meeting the baby. This allows the puppy to develop a sense of familiarity. When you bring the two of them together for their first greeting, hold your baby while sitting in a chair and let the puppy smell the baby's feet and hands. Then allow the pup to smell the baby's head and body. Let the puppy approach the baby, and do not force the baby on the puppy.

The baby will be squirming, making noises, and perhaps may even be crying. These are new sounds and actions for the puppy, and he does not know yet how to process this situation. If, at any time, the puppy seems agitated or jealous, then remove the puppy from the room.

Perhaps take the puppy outside or distract him with a toy. After a few moments, try the introduction again. Many dogs, in general, are excellent with children, but do not accept this generalization as a given. Slowly, over time, the new puppy will be gentle and happy around the baby, and the child will have his/her own personal security guard. This comes with time and patience on your part.

During the infancy stage, you should never leave your baby unattended with the puppy. Any sudden actions or behaviors caused by the baby could scare your puppy, and he may inadvertently injure the baby in self-defense. Because baby toys and puppy toys are similar in style, size, and shape, you should keep the puppy away from the baby toys. Similarly, keep the puppy toys away from the baby. The puppy will not be able to distinguish the difference between their and the baby's toys and could become possessive with all of them. Also, you need to protect your pup from small toys that can be ingested.

You should also not allow the puppy into the baby's room. Secure a gate in the doorway, and train your puppy to wait outside the door. In time, when the baby has grown into a toddler, you should still enforce the rule that the dog stays out of the child's room. When your baby is old enough to sit in a high chair to eat you should not allow your puppy near the baby. You do not want to encourage the baby to feed the puppy, and you do not want to encourage the puppy to try and get to the baby's food. This could lead to additional territorial issues that are more difficult to address once the precedence has been established.

Always reward your puppy for good behavior around the baby. A small treat and repetitive words of praise will forge a strong bond between them. You want to be sure you spend one-on-one quality time with your puppy every day so you do not create jealous feelings between the three of you. With supervised interaction, the puppy will quickly become a well-adjusted member of the family.

Introducing another dog

Introducing your new puppy to another dog in the family also requires a gentle introduction. The resident dog may not be accustomed to another dog in the home and may feel threatened, jealous, or protective and territorial of his environment. It is best to have two people involved with the introduction.

Have each dog on a leash and allow them to sniff each other. Once you see if they are interested in each other, you can unleash them and allow them to further explore each other. It is likely the puppy will take the submissive approach and lie down to allow the resident dog to sniff and investigate. The resident dog may posture over the puppy to establish who the boss is. If you find aggression between the puppy and the resident dog, separate them until they calm down and then begin a reintroduction.

It may take a few days for them to become friends, or they might become friends instantly. During this time of getting to know each other, it is best to not leave the two of them alone. Supervision at all times is the best course of action. A daily routine should be established where the puppy and the resident dog have one-on-one time with you, and also time together with you.

You want to establish trust and boundaries between the puppy, the resident dog, and the family. When it is feeding time, you need to have separate feeding stations for the puppy and the resident dog. They need their own water bowls and food bowls. The feeding stations should not be placed side by side; leave at least 5' of space between each feeding station so you do not find yourself in a fighting situation over food.

Do not allow the puppy to go to the resident dog's food bowl while the resident dog is eating and, conversely, do not allow the resident to try to eat out of the puppy's bowl while the puppy is eating. In the beginning during feeding time, you should supervise the feeding and correct any wrong behaviors on the spot. Eventually, you will not need to supervise feeding times because the puppy and the resident dog will understand their boundaries. You might see them switching bowls during feeding time as the puppy and resident dog grow older and as long as this is a cordial switching bowls, then you will be fine and can allow this to happen. This is an indication that they are comfortable with each other.

Until the time comes where the puppy and the resident dog are comfortable with each other, you need to provide separate sleeping arrangements. The puppy and the resident dog should have their own bed or blanket at bedtime. There will be a time where they may end up sleeping together, and that is fine because this happens on their own terms while they adjust to each other.

If you find you are in a situation where aggression and the urge to fight doses arise, separate the dogs immediately. Do not allow them to fight it out. You need to nip aggressive behavior immediately. It is likely that aggressive behavior will happen while the dogs are off the leash, and you need to be careful to separate them so you do not inadvertently get bitten. Get behind the smaller dog and grab the dog from behind. Lift the back legs off the ground and pull away from the other dog. Swift and prompt reaction time is essential to avoid harm to either dog. It is a good idea to have pepper spray on hand to curtail this behavior, should it get out of hand.

Aggressiveness is not always present and many breeds to not behave aggressively with each other once they are familiar with each other. Still, it is best to be prepared for this circumstance should the occasion arise where aggressive behavior is present. Quite often, the puppy will learn from the resident dog as the resident dog shows the puppy the ropes, so to speak.

Once the puppy and resident dog are familiar with each other, you should expect to find them living in complete harmony with each other. They will become fast friends, and their bond with each other will create a long and healthy relationship.

Introducing a cat

Contrary to popular belief, dogs and cats can get along. They can interact playfully with each other depending on the personality of the cat. Some cats are playful and easy going, some are territorial, some are shy, some are persnickety, and some are downright mean and angry. Unless you have the mean, angry cat, you should have no problem findings dogs and cats cohabitate in a friendly nature.

Just make slow and proper introductions for a smooth transition. If you already know you have a mean, angry cat, then you will need to keep them separated so the puppy does not get injured. It may take a long time before the mean, angry will befriend your puppy, if ever. For all other personalities of cat such as the playful and easy going, territorial, persnickety, or shy cat, these simple introductory steps will help ensure a harmonious household:

- When you come home with your new puppy, leave the cat in a bedroom with the door closed. Be sure you have the cat supplies such as litter box, food, water, and toys in the room so your cat is comfortable.
- Then take a towel and rub it all over the puppy. Rub the anal area where the scent is strongest. Place the towel in the room with the cat so your cat becomes familiar with the dog's scent. Leave the cat alone in the room while the puppy explores the new house and the family. Be sure to let him outside

to void before allowing the cat to leave the bedroom.

Once he has become relaxed and feels comfortable, you can let the cat out of the bedroom. It would be ideal to have at least two people available during the introduction so one person can monitor the puppy and the other monitor the cat. For easier control of the puppy, you should have him on a leash. Let your cat come to him so the cat explores this new intruder on its own terms. The puppy may be scared, but this is normal. The puppy has never seen a cat before. After a few moments of introduction, place the cat back in the bedroom and close the door. Repeat this introduction process several more times once the puppy has begun to relax and get comfortable again. This momentary introduction gives the cat time to process this information. After a few introductions while he has been on a leash, you can remove the leash and let him move about freely and explore the cat. You can leave the cat to roam about the house to do its own exploring. During the next few days, you should supervise all interactions between them.

- During this introduction period, you may see negative behavior changes in both animals. Do not yell at them. Just cuddle and reward them equally, and do this in the presence of both of them so each one feels your love and compassion.

- The puppy will be very curious about the litter box and will eat the feces. As disgusting as this seems, the puppy will think this is delectable. You want to keep your litter box away from the puppy, and you certainly do not want to have such a bad habit develop. It is easier to keep the litter box away from the puppy than it is to un-train him from eating cat feces.

- The best way to keep your puppy from the litter box is to have the box in a separate room with a gate installed in the doorway. This way the cat can jump over the gate to use the litter box, and the puppy cannot gain access to the delectables.
- The puppy will enjoy eating the cat food, so you will need to relocate the food dish to a higher location. You want the cat to eat without interference, and you want to avoid a puppy/cat confrontation at feeding time. You may find that the cat shows interest in the puppy food, so be sure to monitor feeding time with the puppy.

- Prior to bringing the puppy home, you should trim your cats' nails. You want to avoid injury to the new animal. Cats can strike fast, and the puppy will not react as quickly as the cat. Every day you need to allow one-on-one time with both of them so they feel equally loved.
- Over time, and in most cases, they will come to accept each other. They will become friendly. Patience during the introduction period is your reward to peacefulness within your home.

Greeting Visitors

Greeting visitors is a training that needs to start when your puppy is young. If you get him properly trained when visitors arrive, then you'll not have to curtail improper greetings at an older age. Correcting poor behavior is more difficult to change than it is to properly train your puppy from the beginning.

Before you can train him to properly greet visitors, he needs to understand the two basic commands of sit and stay. Begin with leashing him and having him sit beside you when visitors arrive so you can control the situation. Praise and positive reinforcement will help him to remain calm. You may find you need to practice greeting visitors often before he understands that barking, jumping, and hyper behavior is unacceptable. Educate your visitors prior to arrival on how they can assist with the training. Your visitors should act in a calm manner and stay at a distance so the puppy can sniff the stranger. It is not necessary to be in close proximity for him to smell the guest. Ask your visitor to enter the home sideways and walk in an arc around the puppy. Then ask the visitor to sit down and walk him to the visitor to explore them. Do not force the introduction. Let him approach the visitor. If he is pulling on the leash, jumping on the visitor, or acting aggressively, then you need to bring him back to your side and instruct him to sit and stay. This could take numerous tries in the beginning until your puppy grasps the concept. You need to reward him with praise and a treat as soon as he does sit and stay. Once he is calm, begin with the introduction again. Give your visitor treats to reward the puppy and ask your visitor to praise him when the behavior warrants a reward.

Over time, with consistent repetition, your puppy will behave properly when visitors arrive. Once you have complete control of the situation, you will no longer need to leash him when you greet visitors.

Feeding time

Prior to bringing your puppy home, you have planned ahead and bought food, treats, and other supplies. You might be unsure how much or how often you should feed him. For starters, you need to feed him quality puppy food for a year before switching to adult dog food. The puppy is growing at a rapid pace, and the nutrition in puppy food will provide a proper balance of vitamins and minerals needed to support healthy growth. There are several thoughts on how much and how often you should feed him. The bag of puppy food has serving suggestions written on it, and you could follow those guidelines. I prefer to leave some food in the bowl so the puppy can graze when hungry. I have found most dogs eat when they're hungry. They are not gorgers and do not stuff themselves until they become sick. I always set a dinner feeding schedule and serve dinner at the same time every day.

After vigorous activities, allow for 30 minutes to lapse prior to feeding. Resume vigorous activities after 30 minutes has lapsed, once fed.

This is the only time during the day where I add canned puppy food into the dry food. I do not add the entire can into the bowl but split one can into three servings. By adding 1/3 of a can to the dinner feeding, he gets rewarded with a special treat once a day. The reason I do not add the entire can of food to the bowl is because you will find the puppy unable to control its bowels. The canned food creates a wet stool, and he might have accidents in the house. Serving 1/3 of the can does not create this situation, and the stools are solid and normal. Any dog does have a tendency to become overweight if not active enough so be sure to monitor the diet and make necessary adjustments to keep to keep your dog healthy and within normal weight range. As your dog matures, you may need to add nutritional supplements, for overall health, and glucosamine, for joint health, to your dog's diet; it is best to discuss supplements with your veterinarian.

    It is important to have a feeding station for him to eat from. Placing the bowls on the floor for him to eat from can cause discomfort. The puppy needs to be standing to eat, and the food and water bowls need to be at a height where he is not leaning down into the bowls but directly into them. This aids in proper digestion and avoids bloating. Wash the food and water bowls daily, and be sure to have fresh water available at all times.

Treats for your puppy should be used for rewarding good behavior and should be associated with positive reinforcement. You will find your puppy to be most compliant when you offer something special when the treat is associated with responding to a trick or a command. You need to be careful with treat selection because it's quite common that goodies made outside the United States contain poisonous ingredients. I am sure you have heard of treats being recalled because they contain ingredients that can prove fatal in dogs. Sadly, this is a fact. Part III has some delicious, easy recipes you can make for your dog.

For my dogs, I have found Pupperoni@ treats are their favored one over all others. These types of treats are also an excellent way to reward your puppy during training. I only break off a small piece as a reward and do not feed the entire piece all at once. I keep these treats in my pocket during walks to further encourage good behavior outside the home.

On the subject of treats, I feel I need to share this true story so you do not fall victim to the same situation I found myself in once: While away from home, my dog, Beauty, was able to reach a bag of treats off the counter. The bag was already opened, and she went about sticking her nose into the bag to eat the treats. As she got deeper into the bag, her head became wedged inside. She struggled, unsuccessfully, to get her head out of the bag and suffocated.

I was broken-hearted when I arrived home to discover she tragically died over something that could have been easily avoided. Keep your treats stored securely up and away from your pets.

At times, you might want to feed him a scrap off your plate. The puppy might seem cute begging for a treat, but it is not cute once begging gets out of control. If you have food scraps that are suitable for your puppy, then you should put the food in his food bowl. Because dogs have a different metabolism from humans, some foods can be hazardous to a dog. Your dog could experience digestive issues such as vomiting and diarrhea, some foods can cause death. Foods that should not be fed to a dog include, but are not limited to:

- Alcoholic beverages
- Avocado
- Bones from fish, poultry, and meat
- Chocolate, coffee, tea, or any caffeinated beverages
- Grapes, raisins, or currants
- Macadamia nuts
- Milk
- Mushrooms
- Onions
- Garlic
- Tobacco

- Yeast dough

Housebreaking your puppy

Housebreaking him should begin right away. The kennel where he was born should have begun paper training around four weeks of age. Depending on the climate, your puppy may have been spending time outdoors and had the opportunity to get familiar with voiding outside. You should not expect the kennel to have your eight-week-old completely housebroken. This is your responsibility. Most dogs are quick learners, and you should confidently be able to easily housebreak him in a very short period of time. The following tips should help you train your puppy to void outdoors:

- When you bring your puppy home from the kennel, you should expect accidents in the house. Do not scold, hit, punish, or push your puppy's face into the accidental puddle or feces. These are not only poor training techniques; they will instill fear in your puppy, and you will not accomplish the end goal of housebreaking with ease. A simple and firm "no" and getting him outside right away is all you need to say at that moment. Because he just voided in the house, the urge to void outside will not be present because he has emptied his bladder. But, this will give the indication to him that going outside to void is expected.

This reminds me of a man who came to our kennel to select a puppy. The puppies were 5 weeks of age and were already paper trained. The puppies were voiding on the papers, and the man was astonished that such young puppies could be so obedient. He asked me how I did it, and I gave a brief explanation on how I paper train them. He then went on to say to me, "Oh, we never do that with our dogs. We beat them until they go outside." I was disgusted when I heard this and told the man we never hit our puppies and asked him to leave. There was no chance that I would consider selling one of our beautiful puppies to a man that prides himself on beating dogs for obedience.

- Your home is a new environment, and your puppy will be confused in the beginning on which door to go to when it is time to go out. You have kitchen doors, bedroom doors, and bathroom doors. Doors are everywhere. You need to establish which door is the "out" door. To do so, place newspapers by the "out" door. Your puppy will be familiar with voiding on the papers because that was learned in the kennel. When your puppy voids on the paper, do not clean it up. Simply place fresh layers on top of the soiled layers. The objective is to have the scent Linger and it will draw the puppy to that area. Every day for the next few days you should clean up the papers, sanitize the area and start with a fresh layer of papers. Now you have established which door is the "out" door.

- You do not want to rely on using the newspapers as a place for him to relieve himself, this practice is to introduce the "out" door. Remember, the main objective is to housebreak him. You need to take him outside often and develop a schedule. The bladder and the colon are small and cannot hold much waste at this age. The key is to take him out at least once an hour. The most important time to take him out is just after he has awakened. You need to scoop him up and hurry him outside in the very beginning. Do not expect him to be able to run outside to void because he will be urinating all the way to the door. The puppy cannot help it. So, scurry him outside right away and wait for him to void. Then praise, reward, and make a huge happy fuss that your puppy did a great job. It will not take long for him to know to run outside to void upon wakening, and you'll not need to carry him outside very long.

- It is not possible to take your puppy out every hour during the night like you are able to do during the day. To make night time voiding easier, limit the amount of water he has around an hour before you plan to retire. The last thing to do before retiring to bed is to take him outside. At least twice during the night you will need to take him outside. Be firm that this is potty time, not play time.

- Eventually, your puppy will be able to hold its urine and feces longer because the bladder and colon are growing larger in size, and the puppy is learning that he is expected to void outside. You will no longer need to use newspapers by the "out" door. Be sure to clean up your yard daily and continue to monitor him outside and keep him from eating his own feces. As disgusting as this is, puppies will eat their own waste if given the opportunity.

- If housebreaking your puppy seems complicated and time consuming, it is not. With repeated visits outdoors and due diligence on your part, you should have positive results in a matter of just a few weeks. It is common for most puppies to be totally housebroken within just a week. Praise and words of encouragement, along with patience will prove positive!

Crate Training

I have often been asked on my opinion of the use of crates when training a puppy. Although I do not use a crate with our dogs, I do believe that crates have a positive effect on raising a puppy. The crate should be used as a safe haven; a place the puppy can retreat to, which provides comfort and familiarity. The crate should be lined with a blanket and have toys readily available.

The door to the crate should be left open so the puppy can come and go freely on its own terms. If used properly, he will love the crate so much that he will voluntarily enter the crate to sleep whenever it wants to.

You might need to use the crate to keep your dog safe while away from home, and if you make the crate a pleasurable zone for your puppy, you should have no problem getting him to enter the crate when you leave the house.

Always take him outside to void before leaving him in the crate. You do not want to force him to hold his urine or feces for an extended period of time, and you do not want him to void in the crate because you left him in it too long. The puppy will not like voiding where it sleeps, and this can cause a negative reaction to the crate. Once they lose the feeling of the crate being the safe zone, it will not want to go in it any longer. If you plan to use the crate as a way to keep him safe while you go to work, you must make arrangements for someone to come let him outside during the day. If you are able to come home during your lunch break, then do so. Never, under any circumstance, use the crate as a punishment. This is not a place for "time out," and it should never be used in this manner.

When Duke was a puppy, I tried to use a crate on him. He did not want to be in the crate, and he was going to show me he was the boss. He figured out how to open the crate. When I returned home one day after leaving Duke in the crate for just two hours, I found him running all around the house. He had a party!

He got into the pantry and ate potato chips, got into the cookies, into the trash can, and generally made a huge mess for me to clean up. Luckily, he did not ingest anything that could have made him sick. He was so happy to see me upon my arrival home, and he didn't think he did anything wrong. I could not correct his behavior because too much time had lapsed between the breaking out of the crate and the party he had. Moral of this story: be sure to firmly secure the crate door.

Veterinary care

During the first 7 months, your puppy will require a series of vaccinations that are essential to his well-being. The shots include canine distemper, parvovirus, CAV-2 for hepatitis, and rabies. Because the shots take nearly 7 months for the entire series to be administered, you should be particular on where you take your puppy when going on outings. The old saying "an ounce of prevention is worth a pound of cure" definitely applies here. When the puppy was at the kennel, the breeder should have had the first set off shots administered, and you should have received a copy of the shot records to take to your own vet. The second set of shots will need to be administered four weeks after the first set of shots were given. Be certain to schedule the vet visit right away so you get scheduled within the necessary time frame.

Once you visit your vet for the first time, you will be placed on a schedule so the remaining series of shots are given at the appropriate time. While at the vet, be sure to discuss spaying or neutering so you know when you will need to address the procedure. It is wise to have your puppy micro chipped for his safety if he ever becomes lost or stolen.

Grooming your puppy

Keeping your pet groomed is essential to maintaining good health. Begin grooming your puppy at an early age so it is an accepted routine that does not turn into a battle every time you must groom. Nothing is worse than trying to tame an out of control dog when it is grooming time.

- Good grooming habits include brushing your dog daily. It takes about 5 to 10 minutes a day to give your dog a good brushing, and your dog will actually enjoy the experience. My dogs love to get brushed! By brushing your dog, you are removing hair and distributing the oils in the coat.

Remember that the more hair you brush off your dog, the less hair you will have to vacuum or sweep!

- Brushing the teeth is something many dog owners overlook. The germs and decay in the mouth lead to

health problems in the future. Beginning at an early age and getting your puppy familiar with having the teeth brushed makes it easier for you to do a proper and thorough job as he ages. Do not use toothpaste designed for humans. Buy canine toothpaste because it is scientifically designed just for dogs.

Try to brush the teeth at least three times a week for maximum benefit. More often is even better.

- Clipping nails must also begin at an early age so you do not have a struggle with your puppy later. In the beginning you will need one person to help hold him still while another person clips the nails. When he accepts this as part of his routine, you should be able to clip the nails without assistance. You should just clip the tip of the nail. Do not go far down the nail to trim or you will cause your puppy to bleed, and it will be painful. Plan to clip the nails once a month, or as often as needed.
- Bathing the puppy is fun in the beginning. It is cute to put them in the sink and play with them. Soon you will not be able to put them in the sink because they have outgrown it, and you will need alternate ways to bathe him. If you make bathing pleasurable in the beginning, you will create a

positive experience as your dog grows. You do not want to be in a situation where you have an adult dog fighting and struggling at bath time. You want complete control when bathing.

My dogs love getting washed and when they see me gather the supplies to bathe them in the tub, Shelby automatically gets into the tub and lies down. There are many dog shampoo products on the market, but the best product I have found is simply Dawn@ dish soap. If Dawn@ dish soap is good enough to use cleaning birds that are covered in oil from a massive oil spill, then it is good enough for me. It is very concentrated, and you do not need much to bathe your dog. It smells great, and it is cost effective. Just be sure to rinse your pet well. Plan to bathe your dog at least once every 5 to 6 weeks or as needed and don't forget to clean his ears too.

Concerns about dog parks

I am often asked my opinion on dog parks. They have grown in popularity and many people take their dogs there to get exercise and to socialize. I, personally, do not like the idea of taking my dog to play in a place that is contaminated with other dog's waste. There are numerous unknown contaminants in the ground that could also make your dog sick.

There are many people who do not give their dogs proper care and diseases could linger in the waste which could easily be transferred to and contaminate your dog. Remember the Parvo virus discussion earlier in this book? Do you really want to expose your dog to this for the sake of playing? I always recommend finding an open, secluded area to let your dog run free and play. No matter where you take your dog to run and play, be sure to discourage sniffing other dog's feces. This is how disease transfers from one dog to another.

Age to attend obedience classes

You may want to take your dog to obedience or agility classes. The recommended age to train is after all the required vaccinations have been given. This is a standard practice in the industry.

Leash Training

You want your puppy to begin leash training immediately. It is likely that your new puppy has not had any leashing experience prior to you bringing him home. By beginning at an early age, you will establish the ground rules. You do not want your dog to be pulling and tugging while on a walk. It might seem cute when your puppy is small, but it is not cute once the puppy has grown into a large, strong dog. It is more difficult to break improper leashing behavior than it is to install good leashing habits right away. Start with small walks.

    I remember the first time I tried to put my female, Gia, on a leash. My goal was to begin walking several houses away and returning home. Sounds simple enough, right? It was a complete nightmare! She would not walk, and like other children we know, she threw herself on the ground and whined. I tried coaxing her and using treats to get her to at least stand. Nothing worked. I called it quits that day and tried again the next day. Eventually, she got the hang of it. Just be patient and diligent and leashing will become a natural process. You might find your dog pulling and tugging, and you must curtail this behavior immediately. Experts suggest that once pulling starts, you stop and stand still. Direct your puppy to come sit beside you. I know this is easier said than done, but simply just stand there and wait. Do not walk forward until your puppy has come to your side to sit. At the moment of sitting at your side; reward and praise is in order. This will begin the association in the puppy's mind that this is the expected behavior. You may need to practice this many times before the concept is firmly imprinted in its mind. Just remain diligent, and the day will come when walking on a leash is not a struggle.

When leash training Duke, I found that trying to install good leashing habits was a power struggle. He just would not behave. I tried all different tricks to get him to walk properly. Finally, I bought a prong collar. I never used a prong collar and had preconceived notions that using one was cruel. I was quite wrong and am glad I was open-minded enough to give it a try. It worked wonders, and it did not hurt him one bit. From the moment I put the prong collar on him, Duke became a completely different dog. Do not be afraid to try one. It is an excellent training tool for use on that dominate, hard-to-train alpha dog.

Teething and Chewing

All puppies go through a chewing stage while teething. It is up to you to teach your puppy what is acceptable to chew. At their young age, everything is fair game, because they do not know what is off limits. If you see your puppy chewing on something that is not allowed, with a firm "no" simply move him to a different place and give him one of his chew toys. With practice and patience, it will learn quickly what is acceptable to chew. My own dogs never chewed on anything that did not belong to them. Not every dog will chew everything in sight.

    This reminds me of another story: When Duke was a puppy at 8 weeks of age, a woman I casually knew asked me if I wanted a bag of shoes her children outgrew for the puppy to chew on. I was flabbergasted at this. I asked her why I could want to teach my puppy to chew shoes. Her reply was as dumfounding as the offering. She said, "Oh that explains why I cannot get my two dogs to stop chewing our shoes. I never thought about it." Moral of that story is to teach your puppy good habits right away. Most likely, you'll come home and find your possessions in tact because the puppy will eventually learn boundaries.

The Incidental Discovery

The first born puppy with Duke and Shelby was adopted by my daughters, and her name is Maggie. Mags, as we like to call her, often comes over for play dates with Duke and Shelby. The three of them break into a never-ending ruckus and forget all the rules. All they want to do is run, frolic, and play ball. One day when I was playing ball, I was multi-tasking and grilling Italian sausages. The grill became engulfed with flames, and I grabbed my water bottle to douse the fire. The dogs, on the other hand, were running around my legs and dropping the ball at my feet. I was quite agitated as they knocked me into the hot grill.

I took the spray bottle and squirted them in the face and firmly told them to sit. And they sat! Still as can be, they sat and waited for the command to resume playing ball. I had just found a training tool to use during those difficult times where the dogs just will not listen. After squirting them a few times, they began to associate seeing the bottle with, "Uh! Oh! We better behave!" I no longer need to actually squirt them with the water but keep the bottle in their sights. When they are being rowdy, I place the bottle where they can see it and then all is quiet for the remainder of the play date. That, my friends, is my incidental discovery!

Part III

Doggone Delicious Recipes!

Making your own dog food and breaking away from commercial food is becoming more popular by dog owners. There are a number of benefits to making your own dog food and it is no more difficult than making your own dinner. In fact, it can be more nutritious and more cost effective than many commercial foods available. You can be assured there will not be any dog food recalls, as we too often read about.

You can personally select the ingredients in your dog's food and choose the quality of the food you want to use, whether it's food from a local farmer, grocery store, or from money saving bulk sources; you can use organic, free-range, or other kinds of food that you want; this is most beneficial if your dog has allergies. By preparing food in large batches, you can freeze portions for later use, thus saving time and effort.

These recipes were submitted by my Blog followers. They have been taste tested by the pickiest of eaters! These recipes get two paws up, are easy to make, and dogs can't resist how doggone delicious they are!

Pupsicles: Dog Ice Cream Treats

Submitted by Laurie Martin Evans

Ingredients

- 3 ripe bananas
- 32 oz. plain yogurt *NO ARTIFICIAL SWEETENERS! (I use Greek yogurt as it has high protein content. I specifically use Fage Total brand. It has a very thick consistency, very high protein, and naturally low in sugar. Fage is overall a very healthy Greek yogurt brand.
- 1 C. Peanut Butter (creamy) *NO ARTIFICIAL SWEETENERS!
- 1 Dollop of Love (secret ingredient)

Instructions

- Blend the ingredients until smooth
- Pour into regular size ice cube trays, or get creative with other shapes and sizes of containers made for frozen treats
- Be cautious of exceeding a size / volume that will not freeze throughout, or be convenient as a treat for your pup

- Freeze until solid
- After completely frozen it is best to break them out of the trays and store them in a sealed, freezer-safe container to avoid freezer burn.
- Keep stored in freezer

Isabella's Homemade Biscuits – Beef and Cheddar

Submitted by Laurie Martin Evans

Ingredients

- 2 cups 100% Whole Wheat Flour
- 4-6 4 oz. Jars Beef Baby Food (*4-6 jars to have extra on hand in case the dough is too sticky)
- 1 cup Shredded Cheddar Cheese (estimated – as you mix you may want to add more. You want to see the cheese, and your pup wants to taste the cheese!)
- 1 Dollop of Love (secret ingredient)

Instructions: These will be the same for all flavors of Isabella's and Baron's Homemade Biscuits

- Preheat oven to 350° F
- Lightly spray cookie sheets with cooking spray/flour mixture (may not be necessary with non-stick pans, I've done it to ensure no sticking)
- Using sturdy fork, mix flour with wet ingredients
- Start with about 8 oz. of wet ingredient, if seems to be too much flour, add more wet ingredient, an ounce at a time. The best way to combine the wet ingredients into the flour sufficiently is to mix and knead with your hands
- Once you knead with hands and mixture becomes a dough, determine if too dry (add a little more wet ingredient or drops of water), if too sticky, sprinkle in a little more flour then knead some more
- Each wet ingredient (biscuit flavor / batch) reacts a bit differently. You will get used to the ratios and the ingredients you choose. Using your hands to knead is the quickest way to ensure the

consistency is coming together
At this time add any remaining ingredients and knead well
- Once you have a ball of dough that is pliable, but not too sticky you are ready to roll it out. Using a rolling pin, roll the dough onto a floured work station to approximately ¼ inch thickness
- Cut out biscuits with cookie cutters (size appropriate for your dog but not so tiny they burn easily- think no smaller than 2 inches in diameter)
- Place on cookie sheet (they can be placed very close together but not touching – they do not grow) and bake for 20 – 25 minutes

Remove immediately from cookie sheet and let cool (I place on a piece of foil). Your pup will have smelled these baking and want to taste test one immediately – take care, they are hot!

Hints:

Store in the refrigerator. Because fresh ingredients and no preservatives are used, they will get moldy fairly quick if not refrigerated. I keep them in an OPEN zip lock bag in the refrigerator so moisture does not accumulate.

Create your own flavors: Still using the whole wheat flour think about using other variations of pureed fruits, vegetables, and meats as the wet ingredient. You can puree your own, or use baby foods. The possibilities are endless. Always check with your veterinarian about safe foods for your dog before experimenting as some people safe foods, are toxic to dogs.

Isabella's Homemade Biscuits – Apple and Cinnamon

Submitted by Laurie Martin Evans

Ingredients

- 2 cups 100% Whole Wheat Flour
- 12-24 oz. No sugar added Apple Sauce (*extra on hand in case the dough is too sticky)
- Cinnamon (Sprinkle over dough, knead in, evaluate. Sprinkle more if desired, knead, evaluate)
- 1 Dollop of Love (secret ingredient)

Instructions

Follow instructions with Isabella's Homemade Biscuits – Beef and Cheddar

Baron's Homemade Biscuits – Pumpkin and Cinnamon

Submitted by Laurie Martin Evans

Ingredients

- 2 cups 100% Whole Wheat Flour
- 12-15 oz. Pure Pumpkin Pack (NOT PIE MIX) (*extra on hand in case the dough is too sticky)
- Cinnamon (Sprinkle over dough, knead in, evaluate. Sprinkle more if desired, knead, evaluate)
- 1 Dollop of Love (secret ingredient)

Instructions

- Follow instructions with Isabella's Homemade Biscuits – Beef and Cheddar

Isabella's Homemade Biscuits – Peanut Butter and Banana

Submitted by Laurie Martin Evans

Ingredients

- 2 cups 100% Whole Wheat Flour
- 12-24 oz. Mashed / Puree Ripe Banana (*extra on hand in case the dough is too sticky)
- 1/2 C. Peanut Butter (creamy) *NO ARTIFICIAL SWEETENER (estimated – as you mix you may want to add more.)
- 1 Dollop of Love (secret ingredient)

Instructions

Follow instructions with Isabella's Homemade Biscuits – Beef and Cheddar

Simple Summer Treat

Submitted by Laurie Martin Evans

Cut up a fresh pineapple into chunks, or use canned pineapple chunks, and place in a single layer on a baking sheet and freeze. Once frozen, bag the pineapple chunks and serve the frozen chunks as is. This is a perfect summer treat that my dogs go crazy for!

Cassie's Cure

Submitted by Michelle Jezuit

When my dog, Cassie, has an upset stomach, this is what I make for her. She feels better after a few servings, her stools firm up, and she loves it!

Mix one half a cup of Cream of Wheat cereal (cooked according to the directions on the package) with two jars of meat baby food (Chicken, Beef, Pork, or Turkey). That's it!

Moe's Favorite Healthy and Easy Dinner

Submitted by Daneen DeBoth

Ingredients

- 2 cups brown rice
- 1 tablespoon olive oil
- 3 pounds ground turkey or ground chicken
- 3 cups spinach, chopped
- 2 carrots, shredded
- 1 zucchini, shredded
- 1 cup peas, canned or frozen

Instructions

- In a large saucepan, cook rice according to package instructions; set aside
- Heat olive oil in a large stockpot over medium heat. Add ground turkey or ground chicken and cook until browned, about 3-5

- minutes, making sure to crumble the turkey or chicken as it cooks
- Stir in spinach, carrots, zucchini, peas and brown rice until the spinach has wilted and the mixture is heated through, about 3-5 minutes
- Let cool completely
- Store in the refrigerator in an air tight container

Liza's Slow Cooker Chicken Stew

Submitted by Daneen DeBoth

Ingredients

- 3 pounds (boneless and skinless) chicken thighs (about 10 thighs)
- 1/2 cup chicken livers
- 2 medium carrots, sliced (do not peel, skins contain beneficial nutrition)
- 1 cup frozen green beans
- 2-3 cups water
- 1 cup frozen peas
- tablespoon olive oil

Instructions

- Chop chicken and liver into chunks
- Add all ingredients, except peas and green beans, to the slow cooker
- Use just enough water to cover ingredients
- Cover and cook on low 6 to 8 hours or high 4 to 5 hours
- About 15 minutes before turning off the slow cooker, add peas and green beans.
- Allow to cool for about ½ hour and use an emersion blender or a regular blender to break the stew down into a dog food consistency mixture

Moe Loaf

Submitted by Daneen DeBoth

Ingredients

- 1 cup carrots, finely sliced (do not peel, skins contain beneficial nutrition)
- ½ cup fresh or frozen peas
- 1-pound ground beef
- 1/2 fresh wheat breadcrumbs

- 2 tablespoons tomato puree
- 2 eggs, beaten
- ½ cup low-fat cheddar cheese, shredded
- 3 eggs, hard-boiled and shelled and chopped

Instructions

- Preheat oven to 350 ° F
- Steam the carrots and peas until just tender and set aside to cool
- Mix the ground beef with the breadcrumbs, tomato puree, and beaten eggs until well combined
- Stir in the carrots, peas, shredded cheese, and chopped eggs
- Place the mixture in a greased 2-pound loaf tin
- Cover with foil and bake on the middle shelf for 1 1/2 hours

Turn out onto a plate, and leave to cool. Cut into slices. Store any leftover Moe Loaf in the refrigerator for up to a week.

Liza's Sweet Potato Strip Chips

Submitted by Daneen DeBoth

Ingredients

- 1 large sweet potato
- 1 Tbsp. olive oil
- Cinnamon (to taste)

Instructions

- Preheat oven to 250° F
- Slice sweet potatoes into long ¼" thick strips
- Toss the sweet potato slices with olive oil and thoroughly coat
- Place on a cookie sheet, lined with foil
- Sprinkle with cinnamon
- Bake for 2 ½ to 3 hours
- Allow to cool and store in refrigerator in an airtight container for up to 3 weeks; can freeze for up to 3 months

Homemade Chicken and Beef Jerky

Submitted by Sandy and John Ferguson

This is oh-so-easy and my dogs love it! And the best part: no added chemicals!

Ingredients

- 1 pound of boneless, skinless chicken breast or 1 pound of beef (any kind)

Instructions

- Place chicken breast or beef in freezer and freeze just until firm but not frozen, about 45 minutes to one hour. Slightly freezing the chicken or beef makes it easier to thinly slice
- Preheat oven to 170º F
- Remove chicken or beef from freezer and slice as thinly as possible
- Arrange the slices in single layer on a foil lined baking sheet
- Cook for 2 hours
- Once cool, store in an airtight container in the refrigerator for up to 30 days

Peanut Butter Bacon Bars

Submitted by Teri and Mandy Bognar

Ingredients

- 1 1/2 cups whole wheat flour
- 1/2 cup peanut butter
- 1/2 cup melted bacon fat
- 1 large egg
- 1/2 cup cold water

Instructions

- Preheat the oven to 350°F
- Combine all ingredients in a medium bowl and mix by hand until dough forms. Add more flour if the dough is too sticky. Add more bacon fat or water if the dough is too stiff
- Roll out onto a floured surface, to a thickness of just under 1/2-inch. Cut into 1x3-inch bars. Place on a foil lined baking sheet. Bake in the preheated oven for approximately 20 – 22 minutes or until lightly browned. Turn the oven off, flip the bars, and place back in the oven until cool (this will make the bars crunchy)

Makes about 2 dozen treats; store in airtight container

Maggie's Birthday Muffins

Submitted by Teri and Mandy Bognar

Ingredients

- 2 eggs
- 6 tablespoons peanut butter
- 1 apple, peeled and finely chopped
- 1 teaspoon baking powder (yes, this is safe to use)

Instructions

- Preheat oven to 350 ° F
- Mix all ingredients together until smooth
- Grease muffin tin. Fill each tin 2/3 full with batter
- Bake for 20 minutes, or until and a toothpick comes out clean
- Let muffins cool for a couple minutes before removing to cool

Recipe yields about 3 to 4 muffins. Perfect size for a small Birthday celebration!

Zoe's Banana Peanut Butter Freeze

Submitted by Teri and Mandy Bognar

Ingredients

- 32 oz. vanilla yogurt
- 1 mashed banana
- 2 tablespoons peanut butter
- 2 tablespoons honey

Instructions

- Blend ingredients together
- Freeze in ice cube trays; once frozen transfer to freezer bags to retain freshness

Virginia Clark

After suffering through decades of long, seemingly endless, harsh winters in Buffalo, New York, Virginia Clark, and her husband Robert, decided it was time to relocate to someplace warm and sunny. They wanted to live in a place that was more conducive to breeding their dogs.

Packing the meager-less of items, they moved to Henderson, Nevada with their two grown German shepherds, Duke and Shelby.

Once situated in their new home, Virginia resumed her successful 10 year breeding career. She quickly found a vast following of people in Nevada who became interested in adopting her puppies. Virginia knew she would find a warmer climate to work to her advantage because the pups could spend more time outdoors once they were old enough to venture out; an activity hindered by the cold climate in Buffalo, New York. Socializing and training her pups outdoors before adoption is a priority.

Virginia documents the journey of her pups' life daily, from birth through adoption, via pictures and videos on her blog and Facebook page for everyone to see. During her successful breeding career, she has acquired vast knowledge of caring for puppies, and many other breeds of dogs, besides German shepherds. She is often asked questions from people on how to properly care for their new pup and how to care for them as they mature into adult dogs. Virginia is also called upon to consult other breeders and to assist them with finding good families to adopt their puppies.

As more and more people recognized her talents as a reputable breeder, Virginia decided it was time to document her experiences and share with others the valuable information she has learned over the years. Her first book, *A Guide to Puppy Love; Beginner Breeding* was released in 2015 and won the Book Excellence Award for its quality and content. She penned her second book, *A Puppy Love Day; Tips for Bringing a New Puppy Home* which is also award winning. Virginia is now compiling a series of ten books on the most popular dogs in America according to the American Kennel Association. Virginia Clark's books are represented by the highly regarded author and publisher Joyce Foy at A Vegas Publisher.

Other books by Virginia Clark

Award Winning *A Guide to Puppy Love; Beginner Breeding*

Award Winning *A Puppy Love Day; Tips for Bringing Your New Puppy Home*

A Puppy Love Guide; About the Labrador Retriever, Tips for Bringing Your Lab Puppy Home, and Doggone Delicious Recipes

Award Winning *Blitz Your Book to a Best Seller 21st Century* written by Joyce Spizer Foy and Virginia Clark

To follow Virginia Clark:

http://akc-german-shepherd-pups-for-sale.blogspot.com/

https://www.facebook.com/AkcGermanShepherdPupsForSaleNearLasVegasNv

Google.com/+VirginiaClark